BREAD

Dorothy Turner

Illustrations by John Yates

Food

Beans and pulses	Meat
Bread	**Milk**
Butter and margarine	**Potatoes**
Eggs	**Rice**
Fish	**Vegetables**

All words that appear in **bold** are explained in the glossary on page 30.

Editor: Penny Horton

First published in 1988 by Wayland (Publishers) Limited
61 Western Road, Hove East Sussex, BN3 1JD

British Library Cataloguing in Publication Data
Turner, Dorothy, *1944-*
  Bread.
  1. Bread – For children
  I. Title   II. Yates, John
  641.3'31

  ISBN 1–85210–252–7

Typeset by Kalligraphics Ltd, Redhill, Surrey
Printed in Italy by G. Canale C.S.p.A., Turin
Bound by Casterman S.A., Belgium

Contents

Bread around the world

Bread is made from dough which is a mixture of flour and water. The dough is then cooked, usually in an oven.

There are two main types of bread: leavened and unleavened bread. Leavened bread contains

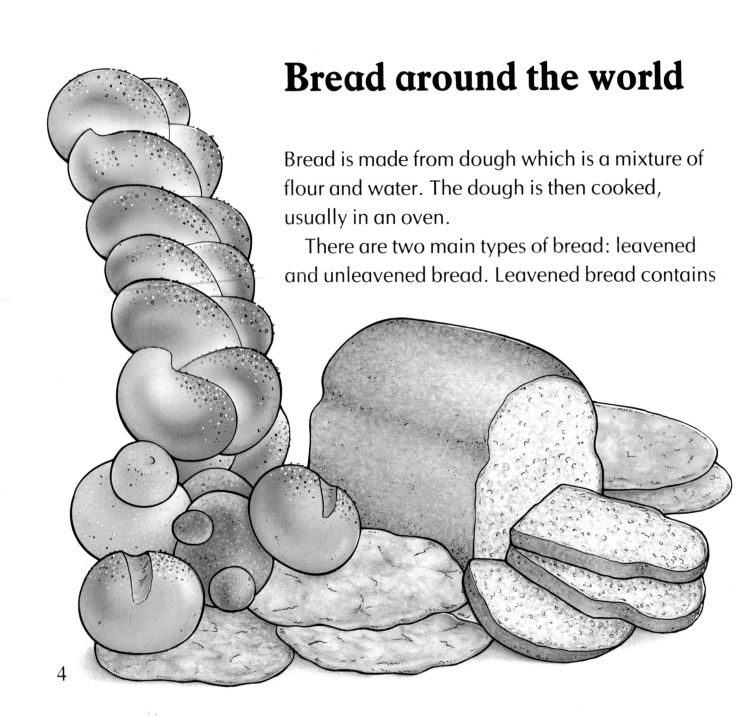

yeast which makes the dough rise. This bread is soft and light like a white or wholemeal loaf. Unleavened bread does not contain yeast. It is flatter and heavier like an Indian chappati.

All around the world, people eat bread of some kind. There are many different types of bread that are made in all sorts of shapes and sizes. Rolls, loaves, pitta bread, pizza bases and French sticks are just a few examples.

The history of bread

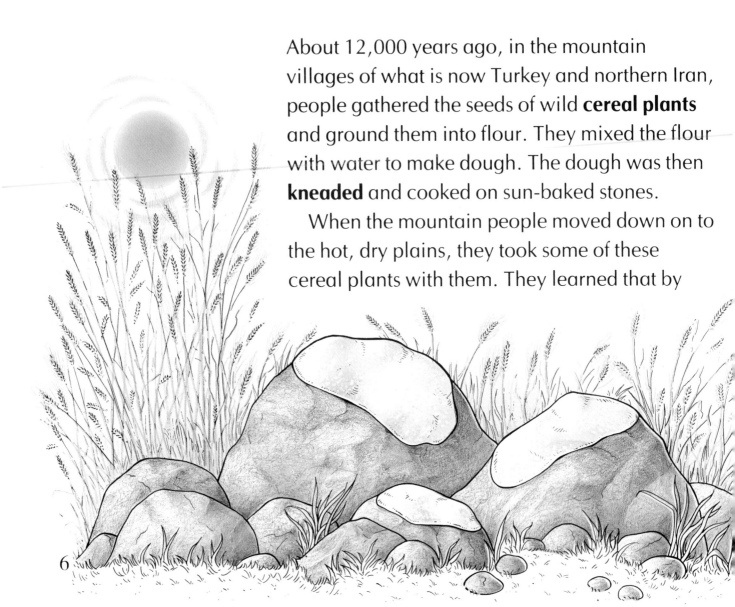

About 12,000 years ago, in the mountain villages of what is now Turkey and northern Iran, people gathered the seeds of wild **cereal plants** and ground them into flour. They mixed the flour with water to make dough. The dough was then **kneaded** and cooked on sun-baked stones.

When the mountain people moved down on to the hot, dry plains, they took some of these cereal plants with them. They learned that by

6

This ancient Egyptian wall painting is over three thousand years old and shows the harvesting of wheat. Flour from the wheat grains was then used to make bread.

Left *Bread was first made by cooking dough on sun-baked stones.*

sowing the seeds plants would grow, and they could use the new seeds to make more bread. This discovery soon spread throughout other Middle Eastern countries, India and Europe.

The ancient Egyptians began to make softer, leavened bread when they discovered that adding yeast to the dough before it was cooked made it rise. The ancient Romans became skilled bread-makers, using many different cereal plants like wheat, barley, millet and rye to make bread.

7

They ground the grain between heavy circular stones called millstones. Their bread was raised with yeast, kneaded, and baked in clay ovens.

Flour was ground in this way for thousands of years. In time, wealthy people came to prefer a lighter, whiter flour. To make this, they sifted the wholemeal flour through sheets of pure silk to remove the rough pieces. Only the rich could afford this expensive white bread.

Above *The ancient Romans used many different kinds of cereal plant to make a variety of breads.*

Right *Bread-makers became more skilled through the ages. This sixteenth-century picture shows the ovens that were in use and the shape of the loaves that were baked at this time.*

Left *The first white flour was made by sifting wholemeal flour by hand, through sheets of pure silk.*

Today, we know that the rough pieces in wholemeal flour and bread are good for us and contain important food not found in **bleached** white bread. As a result, wholemeal bread is popular once more.

Bread made from wheat

Wheat flour is made by grinding up the grains (seeds) of wheat plants to a fine powder.

Some of this wheat flour is finely sifted to remove all the outer **husks** of the grain. This produces a white flour which is used to make white bread.

Right *Wholemeal bread is made from flour that contains the whole grain of the wheat.*

Below *White bread is made from wheat flour that has had the husk of the grain removed.*

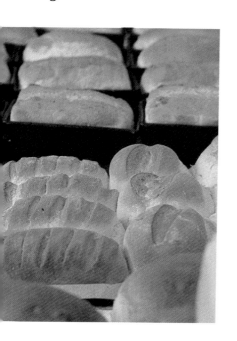

Wheat flour that has not been treated in this way still contains the whole grain of the wheat. It produces a brown flour used to make bread which we call wholemeal. This kind of bread contains more of the wheat plant including **bran** and important **vitamins**.

Wheat is grown in most parts of the world. Huge amounts are grown in the vast **prairies** of Canada and the USA and the **steppes** of the Soviet Union.

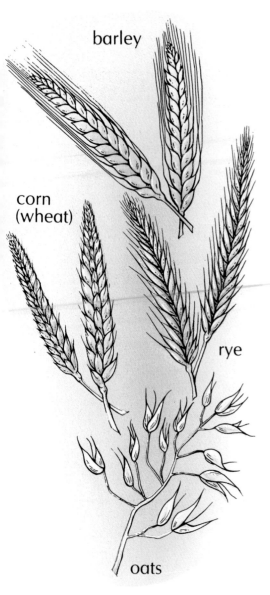

barley

corn
(wheat)

rye

oats

Flours of all kinds

Many other cereal plants can be used to make flour by grinding up their seeds.

Rye and wheat both contain a great deal of a special kind of **protein** called **gluten**. This helps the dough to stretch and rise. The dough can then be raised with yeast to make leavened bread. Rye is used to make a very dark bread called pumpernickel and other black breads which are eaten in Eastern Europe and Scandinavia.

Right *A field of wheat ready for harvesting.*

Left *Pumpernickel is a black rye bread.*

buckwheat

The other flours can not be raised in this way and so they produce flat, unleavened bread. This kind of bread is eaten widely in the Middle East and Africa.

In India, and other countries of Southern Asia, many kinds of unleavened bread are made to eat with meals. Chappatis are just one example. They are circles of dough, thinly rolled out and cooked over an open fire. Chappatis are made from unleavened wheat flour. You can find out how to make them yourself on page 29.

sorghum

millet

Bread as food

To keep our bodies working well we need **carbohydrates** (starch) and fat to give us energy. We need **minerals** such as iron which keeps our blood healthy and **calcium** to give us strong bones and teeth. We need vitamin B to help us **digest** our food and **fibre** to keep the **digestive system** working properly. The seeds of cereal plants contain all these good things.

Below *This diagram shows the amount of carbohydrate, moisture, protein, fibre, vitamin B, mineral salts and fat in an average loaf of bread.*

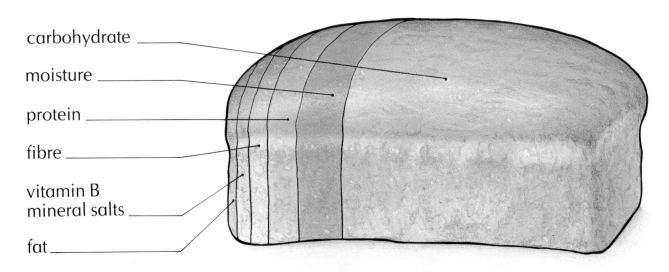

carbohydrate

moisture

protein

fibre

vitamin B
mineral salts

fat

Right *The unleavened bread of Afghanistan is good to eat.*

Below *Bread helps us to grow healthy and strong.*

Wholemeal flour is much better for us than white flour because it still contains all these ingredients. It helps us to stay fit and healthy by supplying our bodies with the essential goodness we need.

Today, white flour is bleached and has most of the goodness taken out of it. Often, vitamins and minerals have to be added to white flour for it to be of any real food value to us. Bread plays a major part in our daily diet, so it is very important to eat good bread to help us to stay fit and healthy.

15

Bread from a bakery

On pages 26–29 you can find out how to make your own bread at home. On these pages we show how bread is made in a small bakery.

First of all the correct amount of wheat flour is measured out and put into a large mixing machine. Some salt, yeast and a little fat are

Below *These boys from New Caledonia in the South Pacific are carrying freshly-baked loaves home from the bakery.*

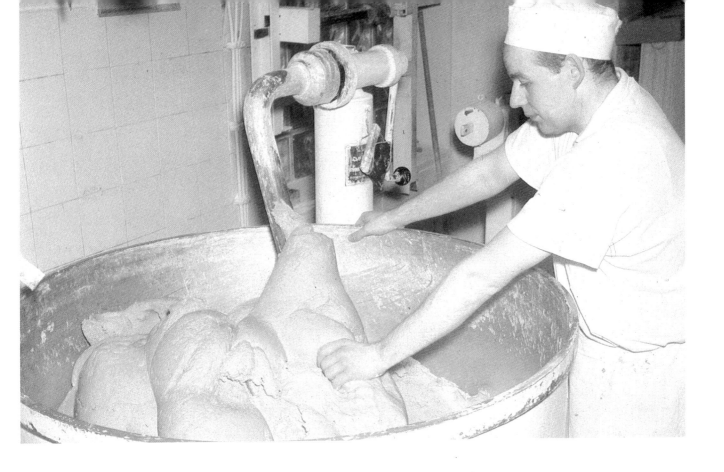

Above *The baker puts the right amount of flour, salt, yeast, fat and water into this huge bowl and the dough hook mixes them together.*

added and then the right amount of water is put in. All this is mixed together and kneaded by a dough hook inside the machine to make a soft dough. Then it is left to rise. We call this proving.

It is the yeast that makes the dough rise. Yeast is a member of the fungus family and is made up

17

of thousands of tiny **cells** which, because they are alive, need food. They feed on sugar and starch which can both be found in dough. When the yeast is mixed into the warm starchy dough it begins to feed and multiply rapidly. As it grows it gives off a gas (carbon dioxide) which forms bubbles in the dough and stretches it.

When the dough has risen for the first time, it is cut into pieces to make loaves. These have to be kneaded to get rid of any big air bubbles. The dough is then put into tins and left to rise again.

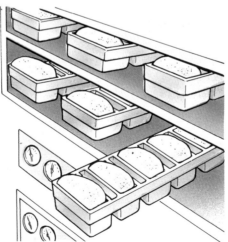

Above *These loaves have been kneaded, left to rise and shaped. They are now ready to go into the oven to be baked.*

After the second proving, the bread is ready to bake. The tins of dough are placed on large trays in a hot oven. The heat cooks the bread and kills off the yeast, leaving the air bubbles in the dough.

When the bread is ready, it is taken out of the oven and left to cool. Now it is ready to go into the baker's shop to be sold.

Bread from a factory

Small bakeries still make and sell their own home-baked bread, but in many countries bread is produced in huge factories. There, the bread-making process is similar to that used in small bakeries, but almost all the work is done by machines. The baker's job is to check each stage as it goes through the machines. Factories can

Below The diagram shows the many different stages of bread-making in a factory.

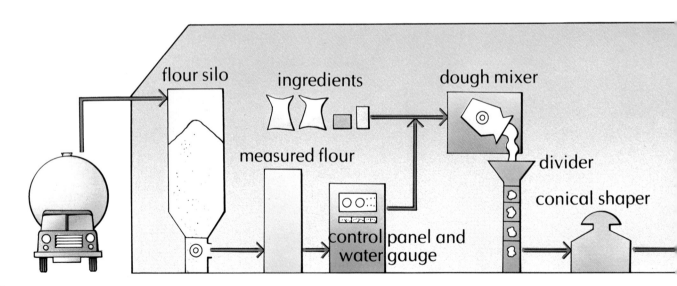

flour silo

ingredients

dough mixer

measured flour

divider

conical shaper

control panel and water gauge

produce far more loaves more quickly than small bakeries. Many of the loaves are automatically sliced and wrapped, ready for us to eat. The finished bread is delivered to our shops and supermarkets in large vans.

This is a cheaper and more efficient way of making large amounts of bread. However, many people prefer to smell freshly-baked bread in their local bakery than to pick up a loaf from a supermarket shelf.

first prover

second prover

oven

dough moulder

delivery to shops

Beliefs about bread

Bread has played such an important part in history, that it is hardly surprising that there are many beliefs about it.

In **Muslim** countries bread is traditionally baked for the feast of Id al-Fitr which follows Ramadan, the month of fasting. The Arabic

Below *In Bahrain, Muslim bakers make vast quantities of bread to eat at the feast of Id al-Fitr.*

Above *At this Greek Orthodox Church, pieces of bread are eaten as part of the Holy Communion ceremony.*

words for bread and life are very similar.

In the Christian ceremony of Holy Communion, bread is broken and shared in memory of Christ's Last Supper with his disciples. The bread represents the body of Christ and wine is drunk to represent his blood.

Bread also plays an important part in the Jewish religion. On the **Sabbath**, a blessing is said over two specially-baked loaves of bread.

Below *Before the Jewish Sabbath meal begins, a blessing is said over two specially-baked loaves of bread. They are then cut and eaten with the meal.*

The bread is then eaten as a reminder that God miraculously provided food for the Jews on their journey to The Promised Land.

In the Soviet Union, the word for hospitality means 'bread and salt'. It is an old custom to give a round, freshly-baked loaf of bread to a guest along with a wooden bowl of salt. This is

Above *A bishop gives bread, as Holy Communion, to the people of the Vai'fa village, Papua New Guinea.*

traditionally a sign of honour and respect towards that person.

There are many legends and beliefs about bread. In some religions bread is offered as a sacrifice to a god. Some people believe that bread can keep away illness. Because of all these different beliefs, bread became so precious that it was regarded as a sin to waste it.

Make sure there is an adult around to help you with the difficult stages.

A recipe for wholemeal bread

This recipe makes three medium loaves of wholemeal bread.

You will need:

¾ litre of warm water
1½ kg (approximately) of
wholemeal flour
28 g fresh yeast
2 tablespoons soft brown sugar
1 tablespoon sea salt
2 tablespoons vegetable oil

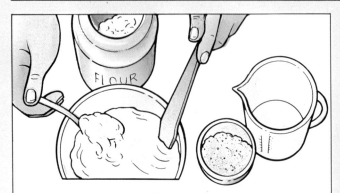

1. Pour the warm water into a large mixing bowl. Add the yeast and sugar. Start to add the flour, stirring all the time until the mixture becomes thick and creamy.

2. Beat the mixture with a large spoon to get as much air into the dough as possible. Leave the dough in a warm, dry place to rise for 20–30 minutes.

3. Sprinkle the salt over the dough and add the oil. Keep adding flour to the mixture until the dough becomes thick.

4. Cover your hands and the work surface with flour. Take the dough from the bowl and knead it into one moist lump.

5. Kneading: Flatten the dough by pressing down and away from you with the heels of your hands. Then fold the dough in half by pulling the furthest portion over the nearest. Repeat these two actions for 5–10 minutes.

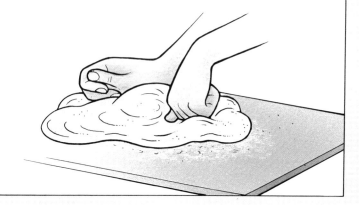

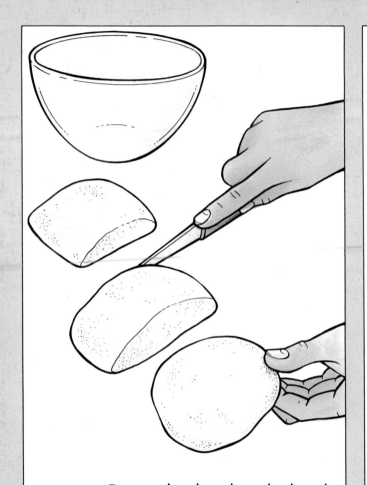

6. Return the dough to the bowl and leave it to rise for 30 minutes. Take out and cut into three equal parts, pressing the cut edges together.

7. Oil three baking tins and fill each one half full with a third of the dough. Bake in a hot oven (220 C, 425 F, Gas mark 7). After 45 minutes take the bread out of the oven and leave to cool.

A recipe for chappatis

To make six chappatis, you will need:

200 g wholemeal flour
½ teaspoon salt
140 ml warm water
a little oil for cooking

1. Mix the flour and salt together in a bowl. Add the water and mix to a smooth dough.

2. Pull the mixture together into a ball with your fingers. Knead it until it forms a smooth sticky ball. Leave it in a covered bowl for 30 minutes.

3. Cut the dough into six pieces. Roll each one out into a circle about 20 cm across.

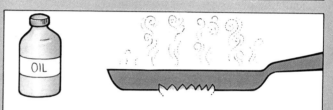

4. Rub a frying pan with oil and heat it until it smokes.

5. Cook the chappatis until they are brown and puffy on both sides. Eat at once.

Glossary

Bleached When wholemeal flour is made paler by adding chemicals to it.

Bran The skin and husk of a cereal grain.

Calcium A silvery-white substance found in teeth and bones that helps them to keep strong.

Carbohydrates Starchy, energy-giving substances found in bread and other foods.

Cells Every living thing is made up of thousands and thousands of tiny parts. These parts are called cells.

Cereal plants Plants like wheat, barley and millet whose seeds can be used for food.

Digest To dissolve food in the stomach so that our bodies can use it as energy.

Digestive system The parts of our bodies that help us to digest food.

Fibre The outer skins that cover the grains of a cereal plant. Fibre is very good for the body because it helps to clean out the digestive system.

Gluten A stretchy kind of starch found in cereal plants.

Husks Outer skins that cover the grains of a cereal plant.

Kneaded When dough is pulled and pushed around to form air bubbles, it is kneaded.

Minerals Non-living substances, such as iron, which

your body needs in tiny amounts for good health.

Muslim A person who follows the religion of Islam.

Prairies The flat, grassy, treeless plains of Canada and the United States.

Protein Any of a large number of substances found in food (e.g., milk, eggs and bread) that are very important for good health and growth.

Sabbath The Jewish holy day which falls on a Friday night and Saturday.

Steppes Large, flat areas with few trees, found in the Soviet Union and China.

Vitamins Any of a number of substances found in small quantities in food, that help us to stay healthy.

Yeast A fungus put into dough to make it rise.

Books to read

The Bread Book by C. Meyer (Harcourt Brace Jovanovitch, 1971)

A First Look at Bread by J.P. Rutland (Franklin Watts, 1972)

Focus on Grain by A. Blackwood (Wayland, 1986)

A Loaf of Bread by A. and D. Lucas (Wayland, 1983)

Making Bread by R. Thomson (Franklin Watts, 1986)

Wheat on the Farm by P. Heeks and R. Whitlock (Wayland 1984)

Index

Picture acknowledgements

The photographs in this book were provided by: Greg Evans Photo Library 11 (top right), 12; Werner Forman Archive 7; Christine Osborne 15 (bottom left), 16, 22, 23; Zefa 11 (bottom left), 13, 15 (top right), 17, 19, 24, 25.